Equipping Your Child for Spiritual Warfare

▼

DR. BOB LAURENT

LIFEJOURNEY
BOOKS

LifeJourney Books is an imprint of David C. Cook
Publishing Co.
David C. Cook Publishing Co., Elgin, Illinois 60120
David C. Cook Publishing Co., Weston, Ontario
Nova Distribution, Ltd., Torquay, England

Equipping Your Child for Spiritual Warfare
©1991 by Bob Laurent
(This booklet consists of selected portions of *Bringing
Your Teen Back to God* ©1991 by Bob Laurent)

Edited by Brian Reck
Cover design by Bob Fuller
First printing, 1991
Printed in the United States of America
95 94 93 92 91   5 4 3 2 1

Library of Congress Cataloging in Publication Data
Laurent, Bob
Equipping Your Child for Spiritual Warfare
Bob Laurent
    p. cm. — (Helping Families Grow series)
ISBN: 1-55513-698-2
1. Christian education of teenagers. 2. Teenagers—
Religious life. 3. Spiritual warfare. 4. Parenting—
Religious aspects—Christianity. 5. Satanism—
Controversial literature. 6. Christian education—Home
training.
I. Title.   II. Series:
BV1485.L38   1991
248.8'45—dc20   91-26538
                                       CIP

*All religions are coming around to Satanism.
We're in the very throes of a new Satanic Age.
—Anton LaVey, author of the Satanic Bible*

*I have given you authority over all the power of
the enemy.—Jesus*

In a recent study I conducted among
teenagers, one of the top eight reasons
given for making a decision for Jesus Christ
was, "a personal encounter with the
occult." proved to be the seventh leading
cause for teenagers in this study to choose
for the Lord Jesus Christ. Initially I was
surprised to find so many teens citing a
reaction against satanic influence as their

entry level into Christianity. Then I began a careful investigation of the escalation of teen involvement with the occult.

After almost two years of gathering data on this phenomenon, I am no longer as astounded by nor as skeptical of observations like this one from Peter Micha, pastor and occult researcher: "It is a fact that, through heavy metal music, fantasy role-playing games like Dungeons & Dragons, slasher movies, etc., between seventy to seventy-five percent of today's teens have dabbled in the occult—and thirty percent of those actually become involved in the occult world."[1]

THE DEVIL MADE ME DO IT

Their attorneys described Pete Roland, James Hardy, and Ron Clements as "good, clean-cut young men," not unlike "most typical high school students." But on December 6, 1987, with their unsuspecting friend, Steven Newberry, they drove to a secluded patch of woods outside Carl Junction, Missouri. After sacrificing a cat to pay homage to the devil, the three teens turned on Newberry, chanting, "Sacrifice for Satan!"

Newberry's panicked attempt to escape

was futile. Armed with baseball bats, they pommeled their friend. Approximately seventy blows later, young Newberry lay dead. With the sacrifice of their comrade completed, Roland testified that he expected Satan to appear and grant each of them great power. Instead, they received life sentences in prison with no possibility for parole.

When the jury inspected a box with their prized possessions in it, they found "a satanic notebook with demonic doodlings, a carved skull with a nail driven through it, and diabolical-looking rock posters and album covers."[2] One attorney stated that the boys' favorite song was Megadeth's "Black Friday," which gloated, "My hammer's a cold piece of blood lethal steel, I grin while you writhe in the pain that I deal."[3]

A few years ago, an incident as macabre as Newberry's murder would have been dismissed as a social anomaly, an aberration that did not merit the public's attention or alarm. The luxury of such disregard can no longer be afforded, according to Maury Terry, author of *The Ultimate Evil:* "There is compelling evidence of the existence of a nationwide network of satanic cults, some branched into child pornography and violent sadomasochistic crime, including murder. I am concerned that the toll of innocent victims will steadily mount unless law enforcement officials recognize the threat and face it."[4]

Many Christian authorities on the occult agree with Terry. "There is a frightening increase of devil worship among American teenagers," reports Bob Sussman, author of *America's Best Kept Secret*. "Over the last few years, there has been a tremendous increase of police reports on this subject in every state of the nation. Some experts claim that it is going on in every community in our country. In one of the most advanced civilized countries in all of history, Satanism is alive and rampant."[5]

Headlines from across the nation attest to the rise of Satanism among teenagers. Houston, Texas: "Devil Worship: Troubled Teens See Outlet for Rebellion." Chicago, Illinois: "Teenaged Satanists Vandalize Church." Norfolk, Virginia: "Satanist, 16, Prime Suspect in Ritualistic Murder." Los Angeles, CA: "Teen Satan Worshippers: Police Confront a Modern Nightmare."

It is becoming increasingly more difficult to dispute the data being gathered by researchers. From the extensive number of preschool cases of the satanic ritual abuse of children, it is certain that "a massive indoctrination of school children into Satanism is going on."[6] We do not have good cause anymore to doubt Arthur Lyons, who writes in his book, *The Second Coming: Satanism in America*, "The United States harbors the fastest growing and most highly organized body of Satanists in the world."[7]

THE SEQUENCE OF SATANIC SEDUCTION

Because adolescence is a period when most people experiment with their belief systems, many teenagers are particularly vulnerable to the mystique and perceived power the occult offers. Until recently, satanic activities have been viewed as fantasy fare for horror movies and the bizarre novels of Stephen King. But now, occult investigators and public officials are unanimously warning good parents that the occult is a viable presence in their children's lives and no teen is immune from involvement in it. A fairly typical pattern for teen entanglement in Satanism has emerged.

The teenager will most likely begin as a "dabbler," or one who takes a superficial interest in the occult. "These ritual dabblers are usually middle- and upper- class teens of high intelligence," says Detective Robert J. Simandl, a specialist in ritual abuse for the Chicago Police Department. He adds, "They are generally creative, curious, and possibly underachievers with low self-esteem."[8]

There are many reasons that youth might become involved in Satanism. Mike Warnke, author of *The Satan Seller*, claims that the Enemy uses the same three techniques to tempt teens as he used to tempt the Lord Jesus in the wilderness: gratification of the ego, gratification of the flesh, and power.[9]

Dale Trahan, program consultant with Hartgrove Hospital in Chicago, believes that teens lured into the occult share two basic characteristics. First, the youth sense that they are "different" from others; that they do not fit in with their "straight" peers. Even though they might be popular, they feels that they do not belong with the regular crowd. Second, they are disturbed by a future over which they have no power. They feel that they are at the mercy of fate and are not in control of their destiny.[10]

Other lures into Satanism include the use of the occult to demonstrate opposition to authority, the imitation of their favorite heavy metal heroes who promote satanic themes (like Ozzy Osbourne, AC/DC, Megadeth, Slayer, Black Sabbath, Venom, Iron Maiden, and Motley Crue), and a dissatisfaction with traditional religion. In fact, teens who disengage from the church are especially susceptible to the occult. Having been reared on a belief in the supernatural, the transition is easy and appears reasonable for them to leave the pious trappings and boredom of organized religion for the excitement and power offered by Satanism. Often feeling that they do not belong in the mainstream, these teens begin to look for ways to meet their needs, alternatives to their current lifestyle.

When youth have reached this point, the occult has no need to brainwash them. The seductive promise of power is too appealing for them to resist. They truly believe that they can get what they want by involvement in the occult. Such teens then explore these new ideas through literature and films found in libraries and video stores. Their changing perspective on life is now characterized by an acceptance of their being different from others ("Nobody really understands me"), a growing sense of superiority ("I have a power that none of my friends have"), and a brooding cynicism about those in authority ("They are all wrong—the church, society, my parents—and I am right"). Armed with this destructive attitude, they begin to seek out like-minded peers.

Once they are involved with a group, the next step of the seduction is initiated, pulling them deeper within the occult. The trap is usually set at a party where free drugs and sex are readily available. As the night progresses, the teen is photographed in some compromising situation. The cult members use the photo to blackmail the teen into signing a pact with the devil. This contract guarantees that the new member will sacrifice himself to Satan at a specified age to demonstrate the ultimate gift to his new master.[11]

Fourteen-year-old Tommy Sullivan, raised in a devout Christian home, signed such a contract with the devil shortly before he committed suicide. His pact read, "To the greatest of demons: I would like to make a solemn exchange with you. If you will give me the most extreme of all magical powers, I will promise to commit suicide. I will tempt teenagers on earth to have sex, have incest, do drugs, and worship you. I believe that evil will once again rise and conquer the love of God."[12]

Young Tommy, whose interest in the occult began when his public school teacher assigned her students to prepare a report on Satanism, crossed the line from being a dabbler in the occult to becoming a deluded collaborator with evil.

SATAN'S GREAT MISCALCULATION

Even though the effects of the satanic movement among American teenagers can be harmful and sometimes even lethal, one of the remarkable finds of this study is that many modern-day teens are compelled toward Christianity because of their negative experience with the occult.

The word occult means "hidden" or "concealed." Historically, Satan's most productive strategy has been to deal in secret, camouflaged and undetected as he "shoots from the shadows" (Psalm 11:2). It has been his practice for centuries to divide and despoil from a distance, always encouraging Christians to fight one another instead of turning their attention and spiritual weaponry against him. Indeed, until recently, mainline Christianity has effectively ignored the existence of the Enemy, and her paltry gains in evangelism are the result. But with the documented rise of Satanism in America, theologians and church members alike are beginning to take seriously the reality of objective evil in the personal forms of the devil and his emissaries.

The machinations of Satan are no longer restricted to the darkness. This change of tactics is most likely prompted by his awareness that we are living in the last days, and his time is short. He has decided to go public with both his forces and philosophies, and in so doing, has declared open war on American teens via black metal music, demonic movies and litera- ture, and peer-induced satanic activities. In my judgment, the devil has made a great miscalculation. He should have left American teenagers to themselves. After interviewing scores of teens who became Christians only after realizing the existence of and truth about Satan, my advice to his infernal majesty would have been to have remained hidden. His exposure has always been his downfall.

Scripture supports this observation. During his ministry in Asia, the apostle Paul openly confronted the forces of darkness.

Immediately after the exposure of satanic activity in Ephesus, Scripture records: "When this became known to the Jews and Greeks living in Ephesus, they were all seized with fear, and the name of the Lord Jesus was held in high honor. Many of those who believed now came and openly confessed their evil deeds. A number who had practiced sorcery brought their scrolls together and burned them publicly.... In this way the word of the Lord spread widely and grew in power" (Acts 19:17-20).

The open unmasking of Satan inspired widespread evangelism among those involved in the occult in the province of Asia. If the following responses of the youth in this survey are any indication, I predict a similar revival among teenagers today—precisely because the Enemy has overreached himself again.

My dad led me to the Lord in my grandparents' living room when I was five years old. But I didn't really become a Christian until two years ago when I had a run-in with Satan's forces. I was watching the movie "A Nightmare on Elm Street" when I suddenly realized that Satan was real. That's when I knew whose side I wanted to be on. It's amazing how God used Satan's tool to change my life!—BARRY, 16

I saw a "Geraldo" special about satanism on TV and it literally scared the h— out of me. The devil worshippers on the show were weird and pretty frightening, but I thought the Christians were pretty cool. One of them reminded me of a friend of mine at school. He's the one who told me how I could be a Christian too.—JIM, 15

I gave my life to Jesus Christ the morning after my best friend and I were playing with a Ouija board at her house. We weren't taking it very seriously—asking the board whether or not we would get married, and what his name would be. It did freak us out a little bit when it seemed like the board was actually giving us answers. But we just decided to blow the whole thing off. That night, when we went to bed, we both could hear heavy breathing, and we were convinced that something evil was in the room with us. I really prayed for the first time since I was a little kid. The next morning, we went right to the youth pastor at our church, who explained to us what was going on and how we could be safe from it. That's the day that both Sandy and I became Christians.—JILL, 16

When people ask me if I've read This Present Darkness, *I tell them, "I don't have to; I've already lived it." I knew that demons were real from the time I was about four years old. My*

father was an alcoholic, so one minute he could be nice and the next he would get really violent. Maybe because I was young, God gave me special insight to see that it wasn't just the liquor that drove him on when he physically abused me and my mother. I could actually see and feel that someone else, someone very evil was inside him. That's probably why I always forgave him for what he did to me, and I know it's why I learned to pray for God's protection.
—PATRICIA, 14

Testimonies like these convince me that God can turn Satan's own strategies against him to effectively evangelize teenagers. There are many things that a concerned Christian parent can do to join God in this battle for the souls of America's youth.

WHAT'S A PARENT TO DO?

1. Exchange your skepticism for a biblically informed commitment to imitate the Lord Jesus' attitude regarding the Enemy.

Jesus said to [the devil], 'Away from me, Satan!' " (Matthew 4:10).

"Adults often don't have a willingness to acknowledge the occult," claims Officer Jorge Fierro of the Allegan County Sheriff's Department. He adds, "Parents say, 'It couldn't happen here,' or they simply choose not to recognize it. Others try to ignore its presence, hoping that satanism will just go away."

Historically, ignoring the existence of Satan has been one of Christendom's more grievous blunders. Widely respected British theologian David Watson states, "The 'enlightened' churches of today, which do not believe in the existence of the devil, are so often lifeless and powerless. They are truly under his power but fail to realize it."[14]

The New Testament is burgeoning with the ubiquitous conflict between the Lord Jesus and the powers of darkness. If He was not commanding the demon hordes to release their hold on the pitiful possessed, then He was directly confronting Satan himself and teaching His disciples to do the same. One can be certain that His heavenly *jihad* directed against the "god of this world" never left His consciousness.

His relentless mission became even clearer the night He was betrayed and handed over to His enemies for crucifixion. He stood alone in the Garden of Gethsemane and announced, "Now is the time for judgment on this world; now the prince of this world will be driven out." (John 12:31).

The Church must never forget that "the reason the Son of God appeared was to destroy the devil's work" (I John 3:8). Furthermore, Paul exhorts us "to keep Satan from gaining the advantage over us; for we are not ignorant of his designs" (II Corinthians 2:11, RSV).

To be ignorant of Satan and his ways is to give him added leverage over us and enervate the mission of the Church. Christian parents must become aware of his devices and be able to recognize his malevolent presence in the world. McNeile Dixon once wrote, "The kindhearted humanitarians of the nineteenth century decided to improve on Christianity. The thought of Hell offended their sensitivities. They closed it, and to their surprise the gates of Heaven closed also, with a melancholy bang. The malignant countenance of Satan disturbed them. They dispensed with him and at the same time, God took His departure."

2. Understand the goal of and philosophy behind satanism.

"Wisdom is supreme; therefore get wisdom. Though it cost all you have, get understanding" (Proverbs 4:7).

In his book, *Michelle Remembers*, psychologist

Lawrence Pasner warns parents that satanism is not secretive about its major objective: complete domination of the souls of the coming generation. "One of its primary aims," Pasner asserts, "is to destroy the belief system within a teenager, to make that youth turn against what he believes in—especially in terms of who God is, and to desecrate all manner of church institutions to which a teen could be attached."[16]

The goal of satanism has never changed. It is the thorough destruction of the temporal and eternal lives of those teenagers involved. It is the complete reverse of Christianity, its moral system insisting that good is evil, and evil is good. Satanism represents the glorification of carnal pleasure. From the Satanic Bible comes its major tenet: "'Do what thou wilt' shall be the whole of the Law."

Satanism intentionally perverts and inverts everything good, discrediting God and glorifying the devil. For example, the redemptive blood of Jesus Christ (symbolized in the communion service) is mocked by teens in satanic cults by drinking the blood of human or animal sacrifices. Communion bread, symbolic of Christ's sacrificial body, is routinely mixed with blood, urine, semen or feces, and then eaten by devil-worshipping teenagers. Often the bread is replaced by human flesh itself.

The cross, signifying salvation among Christians, is used upside down by satanists as a denouncement of God's love. Captain Brian Young of the Iowa State Police reported that one young man who was experimenting with the occult turned every cross in his parents' home upside down in order to curse his family. No one even noticed the act until after the confused teenager committed suicide.

Brian Sussman adds that satanists also believe there is power or energy within humans and animals. This power can be absorbed by the satanists through rituals ranging from sexual activity to murder, dismemberment, or even cannibalism. The satanist's logic (revealing one of the major reasons they target teenagers for involvement) is that the more helpless or younger the victim, the more innocent; the more innocent, the more precious to God; the more precious to God, the greater the defilement; thus the more power for the satanist to acquire. Children and teens are believed to have great energy within them.[17] For Satan, there is no trophy more priceless than a young teenager.

3. Learn to recognize the behavioral red flags of satanic involvement.

"Have nothing to do with the fruitless deeds of darkness, but rather expose them" (Ephesians 5:11).

There are danger signs for parents who are concerned about youth who might be involved with or susceptible to satanism. A teen may be connected to the occult if he or she:

- *is suicidal or has attempted suicide*
- *holds undue fascination with death, torture or suicide*
- *alienates himself from family and/or religion*
- *shows violent and/or aggressive behavior directed toward parents, siblings or authority figures*
- *reveals evidence of self-mutilation (boys on the wrists and forearms; girls on the wrists and breasts) and/or tattooing*
- *abuses drugs or alcohol*
- *experiences a drastic change in grades*
- *has high truancy from school*
- *has a compulsive interest in occult materials, fantasy role-playing*

*games, music, films and videos all
with the themes of death, suicide,
and torture*

- *possesses a "Book of Shadows,"
usually an innocent-looking spiral
notebook with heavy metal groups
and satanic symbols on the outside.
On the inside such a book contains
poems about death, suicide notes,
and the planned date of the teen's
suicide to complete his contract
with Satan. Elgin Illinois State
Police Trooper Jim Vargus, a noted
authority on cult practices, claims
that the book will be written in
code, possibly the Viking or witch's
alphabet. He suggests that other
items to search for are various
ceremonial knives, bones and
religious trappings such as robes,
candles and chalices.*[18]

The teen most vulnerable to the lure of
satanism is one having low self-esteem,
physically awkward, not fitting into a peer
group at school, alienated, isolated, no
sense of humor, sexually confused, bored
and artistic. Vargus adds that there are a
number of satanic symbols of which

Christian parents should be aware.

The PENTAGRAM is the most powerful satanic symbol, uses when satanists seek to contact evil spirits or desire to be possessed by a demon or Satan. The bottom point represents the spirit of man which is pointed down (toward hell). The points represent earth, fire, wind, and water.

The CROSS OF NERO was named after a Roman emperor infamous for persecuting Christians. Characterized by an inverted, broken cross, it has evolved from being a peace symbol to its present status among occult groups as a symbol of the defeat of Jesus Christ.

The "MARK OF THE BEAST" or "of Satan" is used as general symbol of satanic involvement.

The FERTILITY CROSS or ANKH, originally an Egyptian symbol for life and sexual reproduction, is used for satanic rituals involving sex.

The SYMBOL OF ANARCHY represents the rejection of all law, discipline and rules; a popular symbol with heavy metal rock fans.

The CROSS OF CONFUSION is another Roman symbol; it usually signifies a challenge to the verity of the Christian faith.

The BLOOD RITUAL SYMBOL represents human and animal sacrifices; often found at ritual sites.

The BROKEN CROSS or SWASTIKA is a mystic symbol of the Old World adopted by the satanic elements of the Nazi party as their emblem and a symbol of anti-semitism.

The EVIL EYE or "ALL-SEEING EYE OF SATAN" represents Satan's watchfulness and is often used in a cursing ritual; the tear signifies Satan's sorrow that all men are not under his control.

4. Do not hesitate to seek professional help.

"Listen to advice and accept instruction, and in the end you will be wise" (Proverbs 19:20). There is no shame in admitting the need for securing support outside the home. No family with teens in America is free from crises. "Admit your faults to one another," directed James the apostle, "so that you may be healed" (James 5:16). The church is not an elitist gathering of parents with no problems, but a hospice for those who have the courage to face them. Other intervention sources for teens who might be

involved in the occult are as close as your telephone.

- *Warnke Ministries (Information and counseling for occult involvement) 1(800) 345-0045*
- *Teen in Trouble? 1(800) 442-HOPE*
- *Dr. Dale Trahan Hartgrove Hospital, Chicago (Information and treatment programs for teens involved in satanism) 1(312) 722-3113*
- *Cult Awareness Network 1(312) 528-4401, P.O. Box 381, Crystal Lake, IL 60014. This volunteer organization is dedicated to "bringing to the public awareness of the harmful effects of destructive cults and providing information and support for families, as well as assistance to former followers in their reentry into society."*

5. Formulate your own battle plan against the Enemy.

"Put on the full armor of God so that you can take your stand against the devil's schemes" (Ephesians 6:11).

Scripture says that "the whole world is under the control of the Evil One" (I John 5:19). Evangelizing teenagers then is, in essence, reclaiming them from the grasp that the world has on them. Such an effort will not be without danger or difficulty. But the wise parent will enter this worthy battle with several factors in mind.

• The victory is already yours in Christ Jesus. In John 11, Jesus thanked the Father for answering His prayer even before Lazarus was raised from the dead. In the same way, we can be confident that our success over Satan has already been won—no matter what the circumstances may presently appear. "Death has been swallowed up in victory . . . thanks be to God! He gives us the victory through our Lord Jesus Christ" (I Corinthians 15:54-57).

• Your most effective weapon against the Enemy is the Word of God. David Watson believes that the battle against Satan "requires a detailed knowledge of the Bible, committed to memory so that it is readily available for taking immediate offensive action. Every verse of God's Word that you have 'hid in your heart' is a potential sword thrust to put the devil to flight."[19] Just as the Lord Jesus engaged Satan in the wilderness with Scripture, so we parents are to fill our arsenal with God's Word. When battling the Enemy for the allegiance of a teenager, I always find strength in verses like these.

"Greater is he that is in you than he that is in the world." (I John 4:4, KJV)

"Resist the devil and he will flee from you." (James 4:7)

"I have given you authority over all the power of the Enemy." (Luke 10:19, TLB)

"The God of peace will soon crush Satan under your feet." (Romans 16:20)

"And the devil . . . was thrown into the lake of burning sulfur, where the beast and the false prophet had been thrown. They will be tormented day and night for ever and ever." (Revelation 20:10)

•Remember that your success in battle comes from your position in Christ. You must never confront the Enemy on your own. In Acts 19, the seven sons of Sceva, all non-Christians, confronted a single demon without the authority of Jesus. "The evil spirit jumped on them and overpowered them all. He gave them such a beating that they ran out of the house naked and bleeding" (Acts 19:16).

No man outside of Christ has the wherewithal to assault Satan's strongholds. "Apart from me you can do nothing," said Jesus

(John 15:5). " 'Not by might nor by power, but by my Spirit,' says the Lord Almighty" (Zechariah 4:6).

For the believer whose authority over Satan emanates from the shed blood of the Lord Jesus Christ, then God is "a strong tower against the foe" (Psalm 61:3). Such a parent will have "divine power to demolish strongholds" (II Corinthians 10:4) and will learn that "not even the gates of hell will prevail" against him (Matthew 16:18, KJV).

No teenager is beyond God's ability to rescue. And in many cases, God uses the parent to patiently see the teenager through difficult times until he or she is ready to deal with personal spiritual commitment.

PARENTS ARE STILL THE ANSWER

For love is stronger than death. . . . Many waters cannot quench it.—Solomon
I thought of putting my teenage daughter up for sale last year. Did I love her? Of course! Did I like her? Of course not!

I wasn't sure exactly where to place the ad, but the "Help Wanted" section seemed most appropriate. Anyone who is exhausted from daily exposure to the "terrible twos" will come to understand, after one week of living under the same roof with a highly volatile, hormonally charged adolescent female, the wisdom behind the adage, "Small kids, small problems; big kids, big problems!" I remember when our biggest problem was trying to find a thumb-sucking detox center.

Fortunately, there were no takers for my ad. Just when I was about to join F.A.D.D. (Fathers Against Difficult Daughters), my independent descendant left for a visit with a Christian friend of hers in Tennessee. The thoughtful girl who returned to us was nothing like the one who just a few weeks earlier had announced that she hated the whole family and couldn't wait to go to college.

If I hadn't been so pleased by the transformation, I'd have responded, "Okay, kid, who are you? And what have you done with my daughter?" Instead I meekly queried, "So, did you enjoy yourself, honey?"

"Oh, Dad!" she burst forth. "It was just too cool! We went horseback riding and shopping and I met the neatest Christians!"

After a complete debriefing, I realized what had happened. My daughter had experienced an "attitude transplant" during a series of Bible studies with her friend in Nashville. Although she had grown up in a Christian home and attended church from infancy, she had reached that crucial stage of making the Christian faith her own. She had been one of the ninety-five percent of American teens who need an "inner conversion" experience with the Lord Jesus.

I suppose I had for years considered her to be a Christian, mainly because she made a profession of faith at an early age, was baptized into the church, and lived in our Christian family. And yet I knew that sometime during adolescence she would have to face the questions, "What do I really believe?" and "Am I going to live my adult life as a Christian?" That I believed she was a Christian was insignificant compared to the fact that now *she* believes she is one.

Her decision to follow Christ and internalize Christian values made an immediate impact on our home. Before the transformation, conversation with this high school sophomore—when she decided to grace us with her presence—consisted of three grunts and a rolling of the eyes. The house was viewed merely as a pit stop, a place to grab a snack, change an outfit, and borrow some money. Who is this strange "new creature" (II Corinthians 5:17) who let one of her sisters borrow a sweater yesterday and helped another one fix her hair for church this morning? I may not recognize her, but I'm not complaining.

My wife and I are firm believers in the evangelism of teenagers. It can certainly change the atmosphere of a home.

TEENS MAKE WONDERFUL CHRISTIANS

Teens make wonderful Christians because they sparkle and snap with energy. They are perpetual motion machines, euphoric one moment and despondent the next—but never boring. It can exhaust you just to watch their restlessness, but you can feed off it, too. In fact, the parent as evangelist can capitalize on the enthusiasm of youth. Their commitment to a person, an idea, or a cause may appear transient, but it will be all-consuming. In more ways than just those mentioned in this booklet, the wise parent will gently channel this energy in the direction of Jesus Christ.

Teenagers make remarkable Christians because of their sense of humor. They love to make fun of the self-inflicted solemnity of adults. They puncture our pomposity with their quick wit, and are jokingly irreverent about adults, relations, government, their friends, and often even themselves. Youth have a marvelously silly streak, and if we parents just loosen up a bit, we would find ourselves growing closer to our teens while we laugh together over some innocent foolishness of theirs. I am also convinced that if we could dispense with our compulsive concern about good taste, take ourselves less seriously, and cultivate our own sense of humor, we could more effectively evangelize our teens.

Teens make wonderful Christians because they are honest and spontaneous. While questioning everything, they lead us to re-examine our own assumptions and beliefs. Someone once said that "teenagers don't cause problems in the home; they reveal them." Their relentless pursuit of truth inspires and disturbs me at the same time, but I know it is vital to my own growth as a Christian. We really should not think so highly of ourselves. The truth is that while we are praying for and evangelizing our teenagers, they are most certainly discipling us. God uses their candor about religion to shock us out of our spiritual rut and bring us back to authentic Christianity.

Resiliency is a strong characteristic of teens, fortunately, and most of us parents can rely on it. God created them this way for at least two important reasons. First, it helps them bounce back after they have made mistakes, assuring us that there is always hope they can be reached for Christ. Second, it gives parents second and third chances when we fail them. If we try one method of discipline or guidance that doesn't work, they give us another chance. It is difficult to ruin a resilient teen and inflict irreparable scars. Teenagers make good forgivers.

PARENTS ARE STILL THE ANSWER

The survey this booklet is based upon revealed that Christian parents are the key to evangelizing their own teenagers. The number one predictor of teenage faith is parental influence.

The teens in this study cited seven factors (church, friends, youth pastor, crises, media, questions answered, and encountering Satan) as the *immediate* reasons they chose to become Christians. These seven evangelistic entry levels are far more effective if the parents are simultaneously doing "affirmation evangelism" with those teens. Researchers agree that the values of Christian parents exert the most important influence on their teenagers' values. Most studies reveal clear parallels between the children's faith and the faith of their parents.

If parents will focus on four basic areas, the evangelism of their teens will be under way.

1. Christian parents must lead by example.

How is this generation, so suspicious of manipulation, so wary of hypocrisy, to be convinced that Jesus is Lord? There is only one way: they must see Him in us. If we are to pass on the faith to our children, then we must model authentic Christianity. It is not enough merely to be religious or moral. If we are to incarnate the message of Christ for our teens, then we must stand for the same things for which Jesus stood. Jesus championed the helpless, confronted the corrupt, loved His enemies, and eventually died for His commitment to the truth.

Teens have always been attracted to the Cross. They thrive on great causes against impossible odds, and when they observe their parents dying to self and living for others, Christianity begins to look like a cause worthy of their commitment. When youth see their parents refusing to capitulate to the egocentrism of secular society and actively fighting injustice because the love of Christ compels them to do so, they are constrained to consider Christianity for themselves.

Teenagers discover truth via relationships, and parents who desire to evangelize them will focus on the same. The main trouble of youth is not with Christ's admonition to love their neighbors, but with the more abstract concept of loving a distant God. Worship, a sense of what is sacred, a mystical hunger for prayer—these come harder for the young than concern for their neighbors. Of the two dimensions constituting religion—the vertical (loving God) and the horizontal (loving one's neighbor)—they gravitate toward the horizontal.

It is difficult for teens to relate to God in the same way their parents think of Him. The "otherness" of the vertical dimension gives them a problem. And I don't think God minds one bit. In fact, one reason that teens are so reachable for Christianity is that, being extremely relational, they are already close to the heart of God. The Lord could have used many teens I know to write the book of I John. They love its two-fisted charge to make certain that our belief impacts how we treat others. "For anyone who does not love his brother, whom he has seen, cannot love God, whom he has not seen. . . . Whoever loves God must also love his brother" (I John 4:20, 21).

One teenage friend of mine wrote a beautiful account of his belief: "God is to me the Person who gives my life meaning. I could never accept the idea of a God separate and far away, because I know that God really is love—a love that transcends all human differences and binds all people who love Him in union. I also know that the God I speak of is the God of Christianity, because in Jesus Christ, I see the everyday reality of that love."

The Christian parent is someone who believes not in a set of truths but in a person—Jesus Christ. That is what the Christian faith is, and it will never be easy to pass on. There is no infallible formula to follow. But one condition *sine qua non* is that parents possess it themselves. It means living in such a way that our lives would be unexplainable if God did not exist.

2. Christian parents must trust their teens.

The best way to show teens that you love them is to communicate your sincere trust in them. The Bible says "if you love someone you will be loyal to him no matter what the cost. You will always believe in him, always expect the best of him, and always stand your ground in defending him" (I Corinthians 13:7, TLB). Adults will more effectively evangelize the next generation by treating them like adults.

Of course there are risks involved in giving freedom to teenagers. Parents are painfully aware of the damage teens can do to themselves if they are given indiscriminate liberty. But overprotectiveness and smothering solicitousness are tendencies against which youth have always had to protect themselves from well-intentioned parents. The fact is that the apprehensive, controlling Christian parent is the very one who, more often than not, drives the teenager away from the faith.

Parents who are hopeful and trusting are much better evangelists than those who are perpetually suspicious and doubting. Research shows that teens feel closer to parents who create an atmosphere of trust and acceptance, of hopefulness and flexibility. Such parents know that inherent dangers come with trust, but they accept them because they realize that New Testament evangelism is historically a "high-risk/high-reward" phenomenon. Though teens can wound themselves on freedom, their imminent salvation makes the risk worthwhile.

There is, of course, a sense in which teens should earn your trust and be given every opportunity to do so. But many youth have become trustworthy as a direct result of being trusted by their parents even when those teens didn't believe in themselves. The wise parent seeks the balance between earned and unmerited trust, never forgetting that the teen who can be trusted is more likely to be the one who eventually trusts in Christ.

3. Christian parents must learn to take the spiritual pressure off their teenagers.

No one can be forced into Christian commitment. By its very nature, religious commitment is a decision that can only be made willingly, free from manipulation or coercion.

That you thrive on 5:30 a.m. devotions does not mandate that your teen must be a spiritual giant before breakfast. Just because you have chosen full-time ministry as a vocation, your children should not be badgered into following suit and belittled if they do not. You regret your choice not to go to the mission field, but it is as unfair as it is unproductive to expect your child to go in your place.

Parents who persist in keeping on the pressure should not be surprised to find their teens eventually rejecting the faith. Many teens feel that spiritually coercive parents really do not love them for who they are.

Recently a college freshman who was struggling with her faith confided in me, "I know that my mother is worried about me, but I am so sick of her preaching. She phones me under other pretenses, but I'm always waiting for the sermon that she'll slip in somehow. She cannot talk to me as a person; she's always got to bring God into the conversation. She might think that she loves me, but I'm getting the message that she'll only truly love me when I'm the good little Christian girl that she wants me to be."

Dr. David Elkind, author of *All Grown Up and No Place to Go*, reminds us that, when confronted by spiritual pressure from parents, younger children blame themselves for not measuring up to standards. Elementary school children will usually blame the world for their duress. But adolescents blame their parents.

The wisest course for Christian parents

is to stop worrying about their teens and trust them to the Lord's care. Worry is not only irrelevant and irresponsible, it is irreverent. Anxiety over the spiritual welfare of our children, as accepted and widespread as it is in the church, still precludes God's ability to bring them to faith. When I finally decided to follow God's advice, "Don't worry about anything; instead pray about everything" (Philippians 4:6, TLB), the spiritual attitudes of all the teens in our home improved dramatically.

4. Christian parents must learn how to love and be loved.

I was not raised in a Christian home, so it is no surprise that my father and I were never close—a fact that has caused me a lot of guilt and occasionally crippled my spiritual growth. Not having experienced the type of love I felt I needed as a teen, predictably I have struggled with receiving love from my heavenly Father.

Those who get to know me recognize early on that it is far easier for me to give than receive, a personal trait that has plagued me for years and made it difficult to establish close friendships. The sense of low self-worth I inherited as a teen followed me into my adult years and marked each relationship with the same lack of intimacy I'd had with my father. I would let friends get only so close before I would withdraw, convinced that the more they knew me, the less they would like me. One day, out of frustration, a pastor friend bravely exhorted me, "Bob, I think I finally understand you. You desperately need to be loved, and the irony is that you won't really let anyone love you. My guess is that your biggest problem is that you won't let God love you! Every relationship you have would improve if you could get this fixed."

His words cut me to the quick, and I knew that he was right. There had been times when even the intimacy I had with my own children had been bittersweet, a reminder of what I'd missed as a child. Still, I had little confidence that I could change. This friend encouraged me in my devotional life to focus on Scriptures that spoke of God's love for me. I sincerely wanted to *experience* wonderful passages like Ephesians 3:17-19: "And I pray that you, being rooted and established in love, may have power, together with all the saints, to grasp how wide and long and high and deep is the love of Christ, and to know this love that surpasses knowledge."

But not until last Christmas did the Holy Spirit bring the kind of healing I needed to realize the fullness of God's love. We had invited my parents to spend the holidays with us, and as usual, I had mixed emotions. I loved my father, but the distance that marked our relationship during my teen years had only gotten worse as I approached middle age.

I felt that he had always been my critic, austere and disapproving, and I was seldom comfortable around him. I had convinced myself that he did not love me, and even if he did, it never crossed my mind to try to understand why he was unable to express it. Never mind that he was raised as an orphan in a non-Christian home and had ample reasons for not being able to articulate his love to his children. I was determined to hold onto my self-pity and sense of regret.

It is a common complaint among teenagers that their parents insist on treating them like children and refuse to recognize their maturation. During my parents' visit at Christmastime, I learned that the reverse can also be true: many parents could justly complain that their children have categorized them and dismissed the possibility that they can change. I had long ago resolved not to look for love from my father.

Although we both became Christians after I left home, we frequently argued over personal beliefs. Eventually we began to avoid each other, and I felt we had a tacit agreement to steer clear of anything resembling a serious talk. But during his holiday visit, my father broke that contract . . . and I know my life will forever be changed.

I was about to join the family for our annual viewing of *It's a Wonderful Life* when I noticed Dad sitting alone at our dining room table reading his Bible.

"Hey, Dad, the movie's about to start. Let's go downstairs."

He looked up and replied, "Listen, son. I can't do that. We need to have a talk first."

At that moment, I was no longer a forty-three-year-old Bible professor with three teens of his own. It was a boy of fourteen who had just been summoned by his father for a lecture.

But this man, whom I realize now I hardly knew, looked me directly in the eyes and related a simple story. His words were measured, but charged with emotion.

"When I was at Mayo Clinic this summer, I realized there was a chance I might not survive the surgery I was facing. My attending physician was a Christian and asked me one day why I seemed troubled. I told him that if I died, my only regret would be that, although I became a Christian late in life and have had a wonderful ministry, my own son dislikes me."

As he spoke, I sensed that these thoughts were even more difficult for him to express than they were for me to hear. And so I quietly listened, forcing myself to meet his eyes.

"My doctor and I talked for awhile, and then he advised, 'Mr. Laurent, I think you offended your son while you were raising him, and you need to ask his forgiveness.' "

Realizing what he was about to do, I remember thinking, *I'm not ready for this! How am I supposed to react?*

Dad rose from his chair and stepped toward me. "Son, I know now that I hurt you deeply through the years, and though I don't deserve it, can you find it in your heart to forgive me?"

I will never be able to describe the emotions I was feeling just then. But one thing I knew for certain: he was a brave man, and I was proud of him for taking this risk. Still, I was too stunned to speak, so he filled the silence.

"There's one other thing I've been wanting to tell you, son, but I never knew how." With a quivering voice, he said, "I love you, Bob."

My tears were instantaneous. The embrace that followed will always be a prized memory for me. Months later, I am still experiencing the spiritual exhilaration and healing that resulted from our reconciliation.

Simon Peter was right when God inspired him to write, "Love each other deeply, because love covers over a multitude of sins" (I Peter 4:8). Love is the key for reaching your children. Christian parents who have close friendships with their teens make the ultimate evangelists. And the good news is that as the parent of a teenager, you can save the precious years that my father and I tragically wasted. Your love for your teens will lead them to Christ, and in Christ they will not only find life but a parent who is their best friend.

ENDNOTES

1. Bob Sussman, "America's Best Kept Secret: A Look at Modern-day Satanism," video documentary, 1990.
2. Bob Larson, *Satanism: The Seduction of America's Youth*, New York: Thomas Nelson Publishers, 1989, 103.
3. Ibid.
4. Maury Terry, *The Ultimate Evil*, Garden City, New York: Doubleday and Company, Inc., 1987, 511.
5. Bob Sussman, *America's Best Kept Secret*.
6. Ibid.
7. Arthur Lyons, *The Second Coming: Satanism in America*
8. Deborah J. Mayberry, "The Seduction of Satanism," *Notes 'N News*, Vol. II, Issue 10, October 1990, 16.
9. Mike Warnke, *The Satan Seller*, 144
10. Deborah Mayberry, "The Seduction of Satanism," 16.
11. Ibid.
12. Bob Larson, *Satanism*, 103.
13. Dale Dieleman, "Danger of the Occult Is Real," *The Grand Rapids Press*, 14 October 1990, 1.
14. David Watson, *Hidden Warfare: Conquering in the Spiritual Conflict*, (Kent, England: STL Books, 1972), 72.
15. McNeile Dixon, quoted by F. J. Rae in "The Expository Times," Vol. lxvi, 215.
16. Bob Sussman, *America's Best Kept Secret*.
17. Ibid.
18. Deborah Mayberry, 17.
19. David Watson, *Hidden Warfare*, 113.

ABOUT THE AUTHOR

For more than 20 years, Dr. Bob Laurent has ministered to teens. He holds a Ph.D. in Religious Education, specializing in adolescent psychology. Dr. Laurent is the author of *Keeping Your Teen in Touch with God* and the recently released *Bringing Your Teen Back to God*. He currently teaches Bible at Judson College in Elgin, Illinois, where he lives with his wife, Joyce Ann, and their four children.

HELPING FAMILIES GROW SERIES

❦ *Communicating Spiritual Values Through Christian Music*

❦ *Equipping Your Child for Spiritual Warfare*

❦ *Family Vacations That Work*

❦ *Helping Your Child Stand Up to Peer Pressure*

❦ *How to Discover Your Child's Unique Gifts*

❦ *How to Work With Your Child's Teachers*

❦ *Helping Your Child Love to Read*

❦ *Improving Your Child's Self-Image*

❦ *Preparing for Your New Baby*

❦ *Should My Child Listen to Rock Music?*

❦ *Spiritual Growth Begins at Home*

❦ *Surviving the Terrible Teenage Years*